THE SMALL BUT ULTIMATE BOOK OF ONLINE SAFETY

FOR EVERYONE

NIDHI ARORA

Made with ♥ on the Notion Press Platform
www.notionpress.com

For

Mom, Miki, and Ishaan

Contents

Foreword

700,000 *– Number of complaints received by the national helpline – 1930 – in one month. That is* ***16 cases of fraud per minute.***

10,319 crores *– according to Mr. Rajesh Kumar, CEO of India Cyber Crime Co-ordination Center (I4C), the amount involved in these frauds from April 2021 to January 2024.*

Cybercrime is the fastest growing category of crime in India. Arguably, in most parts of the world.

From small mom and pop stores of individual hackers, it has now become a mainstream, organised, and syndicated industry of behemoths and state actors. There are clusters at places like Jamtara and Nuh, and more clusters are emerging rapidly.

At the receiving end of these crimes are normal people. Some lose their identity, some their life savings, and some, their whole lives.

When a company faces a cyber-attack, an army of professionals steps in to help. Knowledge Center articles are written and circulated among cyber security professionals to ensure that the incident is not repeated.

But when a citizen loses money to cyber fraud, there is no army. The police are overworked and understaffed, and hindsight, in spite of being perfect, does not recover the loss. Everyone gets to know AFTER the incident that this is a common modus operandi. These people who lose money are our family members. It was time for someone to write a book to forewarn. It was time to convert hindsight to foresight. This book does just that.

This book has been written after the analysis of hundreds of cases of cybercrime against citizens. If it protects even one person, our work is done.

Nidhi

June 2026

Preface

All of us understand that cyber security is important. But have we ever wondered HOW scams worth crores are successful? What are the vulnerabilities that are actually exploited by criminals?

If you search online for "How to save oneself from cyber fraud" you will get the same 8-10 tips – 2FA (two Factor Authentication), password manager, no personal information, etc.

All that is fine. But HOW do we keep our data secure?

This book fills that important void. It gives practical tips for Indians.

The best way to use this book is to:

Read Section A first – WHY do we need to safeguard our data, and things that can be done using our data.

Read Section B, and follow one tip at a time. For instance, don't give your phone number at retail stores and see how your spam calls come down within weeks.

You might also be able to share some tips with us. Do share them for inclusion (with your name, of course) in the next edition. Email me at authnidhi@gmail.com.

Wishing all of us a safe future!

First Edition: May 2024
Second Edition: June 2024
Third Edition: July 2024
Fourth Edition: October 2025
Fifth Edition: June 2026

Acknowledgements

This book owes its existence to a person I do not know – Security Monkey. He started writing about cases of technology-led crimes almost two decades ago. His cases were engaging and marked the start of my interest in cyber-security.

Gratitude is due to:

The journalists who write reports on cybercrime. The numbers made me realise the magnitude of the issue. An analysis of the stories led to the identification of common threads that are being presented in this book.

To Ishaan, for his constant encouragement.

To my editor, Jalpa Shah.

Author's Note

Dear Readers

First of all, THANK YOU for taking this book to the #1 place - not once, but TWICE on the Amazon Bestsellers List.

The response to the book has been overwhelming.

Thank you for your faith. This has placed an ongoing responsibility upon me.

I promise to keep this book updated. As new frauds emerge, I will add them to this book.

If you have experienced a fraud that is NOT covered in this book, please do share it with me:

@authnidhi on Instagram, or

authnidhi@gmail.com.

It will appear with your name in the book.

Staying Safe Together!

ONE

Why Cyber Security Matters

If a thief comes to you and asks for your jewellery, you will not take it out and give it to them, right?

For decades, experts have been telling us that data is the new oil. So, why are we still giving our data away without a second thought? ***Data is called the new oil because it is a wealth generator.***

Many people make the mistake of thinking that the only use of data is for targeted advertisement. It is not. Data is used for many things, and targeted advertising is the LEAST important of those uses.

Why is Data the New Oil?

Data is used for:

A. Regime change

B. Civil unrest that almost led to an internal emergency (I think, in more than ten countries in the last three years alone)

C. Financial fraud (amounting to a few hundred crores per week in India)

D. Physical crime

E. Targeted spear phishing attacks on enterprises

F. Addiction algorithms in apps, websites, and games

G. Blackmail

H. And yes, getting a few rupees out of your pocket through targeted advertising.

You might have read many stories of cyber hacking or cyber fraud. You may also have got such calls yourself. You might think that these are random incidents in which innocent civilians got victimised.

They are not. ***There is proper segmentation, targeting, and then attack.*** *So, if you have been scammed or have received a scam call, a lot of homework has already been done. Much of that homework is now automated.*

But the average Indian is not tech-savvy. So, how do we protect ourselves from this?

I have worked to create a list of simple things people can do to minimise their risk of being targeted. ***Each of these is a small, simple step that will take you one step towards safety. The***

book itself is small and easy to read, but it encompasses thousands of crores worth of preventable scams. *And that is not an exaggeration.*

Like good health practices, these are good cyber health practices.

TWO

Identity Theft

If you think identity theft is rare, think again.

According to the Crime in India 2022 report released by the National Crime Records Bureau, 5,740 cases of identity theft were recorded.

However, of all types of cybercrime, this is easily the most damaging. Identity theft is pure hell. Identity theft means someone can take loans on your behalf, write messages to your contacts, take over your friendships, and lead to potentially disastrous consequences professionally.

With identity theft, someone can basically take over an aspect of your life. There is the case of a blogger who lost his identity, his access to his own blog, his Apple ID, all within a matter of hours. Another lady had cash withdrawn from her account, and a credit card applied and approved[1]!

[1] *https://www.businessinsider.in/tech/news/a-woman-who-got-locked-out-of-her-apple-account-minutes-after-her-iphone-was-stolen-and-had-10000-taken-from-her-bank-account-says-apple-was-not-helpful-at-all/articleshow/98255581.cms*

1. Do not give your Aadhar Card anywhere. If they ask for Aadhar, ask them - "Do you need my Aadhar, or do you need a photo ID/address proof?" For both these purposes, a Driving License works just as well.

2. When submitting your ID card anywhere, blacken a part of the ID number OR DoB (Date of Birth) so that the ID proof cannot be copied. Especially while checking into hotels and giving ID proof for forms, where it is likely to be handled by a call centre.

3. Do not use runners or other facilitators who can get access to your ID documents. No one should see your ID document unless it is absolutely necessary.

4. Your phone number and your email address are your identity. Do not give out your phone number at office gates, parking lots, and other random places. Keep two phones - one for all personal interactions and one for places where one has to give the phone number. Never share your personal phone number or personal WhatsApp number randomly. Same for personal email addresses. **Phone numbers and email addresses are the foundation stones of identity theft. Identity theft is very difficult without them.**

5. Every account you make on any website is a potential identity theft window. If it is possible to use a web service or app without creating an account, do that. Otherwise, only create accounts if you are very sure you are going to use the service regularly. We have observed identity thefts of people who sign up for a service but don't use it regularly. So, if you are not using a website, make the effort to delete your account.

6. **Doxing** is the practice of leaking a person's address or other personal information on the internet. But many times, we **dox ourselves**. If you are posting your pictures

on the internet (no matter how closed the group), do not stand in front of places that are near your house and easy to identify. If taking a picture at home, try and do it against a neutral wall, without showing any part of your furniture.

7. If you can, keep one number linked to your Aadhar and another number for all communications. If the phone linked to Aadhar is lost, getting the SIM reactivated is very difficult. So, it is advisable to not use the phone linked to Aadhar in public or vulnerable places.

THREE

Financial Fraud

Of all the kinds of cyber fraud, financial crime is easily the MOST prevalent one. According to the 2022 Crime in India report, out of a total of 65,893 cases of cybercrime, 17,470 cases were financial in nature. That is 26%!

These tips encapsulate the most used behavioural vulnerabilities in financial fraud.

1. If something appears too good to be true, it is. This applies to things you are trying to sell, investment options, and everything else related to money. New asset classes are not bad, but ensure that you understand them perfectly before investing.

2. Do not use the same signature for bank cheques and everyday activities. Have two signatures - the official one, and a short signature. When signing for a courier or at an entry gate, use your short signature. Only on official documents, use your official signature.

3. Do not keep money in current and savings accounts. Do not link Fixed Deposits to current and savings accounts. Budget for putting your cash requirements for a month or a fortnight, and put the rest away - even a short-term FD will do. Just make sure that it is not linked to your main account.

4. If you are a senior citizen getting inbound transfers of money from your children, ensure that you receive the remittances in 2-3 different bank accounts, and use the non-linked FD principle to manage the cash. Senior citizens with significant inward remittances are considered easy targets by fraudsters.

5. Do not click on any link on WhatsApp or SMS. Open links only on a large screen laptop, where it is easier to spot fake websites and check http and https: (among other things).

6. Do not save credit card information on any website. Most websites are sneakily designed to get you to store your credit card information. While tokenisation is supposed to make this safe, it is not foolproof. It only takes one extra minute to input your information manually each time. Do it.

7. If an app is available as a website, use that. Facebook, LinkedIn, Twitter are all available as mobile websites. Every app is a backdoor entry into your phone and any one of these apps can be compromised or hacked to get into multiple devices at one go.

8. If you have not used an app for more than two months, uninstall it. When you need it again, you can

install it again.

9. To the extent possible, don't use free apps for things that should cost money - video editing, photo editing, document scanning, are all backdoors into your data. Remember Camscanner? It was a popular scanning app that turned out to be .. well, not just a scanning app. It was subsequently banned in India.

10. In addition to 2FA (2 Factor Authentication), keep different security questions for each banking/ financial app. This ensures that even if one of your accounts is compomised, the others are not.

11. Do NOT share your phone number while billing at retail outlets. They will customarily ask you for the phone number. Customarily say, 'Please bill without the phone number." - this one step will minimise the spam calls you get AND your being a potential target for bank fraud.

12. Do not use the Autofill and Save Password feature in any browser. Do sign out after every single use.

13. Always set your browser to delete all cookies when you close the browser.

14. Do NOT use Google to find service numbers for anything. The number of scams that have happened because Google does not control who can post as a service agency for any brand, is very, very high. Google is not a reliable directory. Make an effort to go to the website of the manufacturer or service provider, and ensure that the website is legit.

15. Don't contribute to crowdfunding campaigns for medical care if they ask for your email id and phone number. Just remember the days when you could leave the house, buy the stuff you needed, attend tuition classes, visit a doctor, and come home, without sharing information about yourself. At most, the doctor took your name, age, and gender. That was it. No email id, no phone number.

16. If you get a message that KYC (Know Your Customer) is pending - Visit the Bank. This is for two reasons - One, you need to submit KYC documents physically, and two, the relevant person in the branch will do this. Do not respond to SMSs asking for KYC to be done online. If you have not used Central KYC, do that.

17. If you use mobile apps for financial transactions like banking, trading, etc., it makes sense to use a phone that is not used for other communication like regular phone calls, WhatsApp, etc. Use this phone only for secure financial transactions. This way, even if there is malware for any reason on your main phone, the financial apps will not be impacted because they are on a secure phone.

18. **Read this tip VERY carefully. Most frauds in the last few years have been one of these:**

No one pays 50 rupees to like YouTube videos.

No company's HR is looking to hire you without an interview process.

No hiring company needs processing fee of a few thousands.

No "task-based" work should need a deposit.

No FedEx courier containing drugs has arrived for you, even if the policeman is talking to you on a video call.

There is no work from home for writing out documents, liking videos, following someone on Insta, or clicking on links.

In short, there are no free lunches. No international role is waiting for you if your "employer" is asking you to pay the visa processing fee to them. Even if the employer wants you to get the visa, they will ask you to get the visa and then apply to them. They will never take your money to process your visa.

19. Your friend/boyfriend/partner/fiance(e) you met on an online platform is not scared for their lives. You cannot save their lives by paying money.

20. When you get a high returns scheme, always withdraw more than you put in. For instance, if you see 10% returns, first withdraw the principal and continue only with the returns. Once the scamsters realise you are taking real money out, they will convince you to exit the scheme quickly. (On that note, there is NO get-rich-quick scheme. No pyramid schemes work, and no smart money manager will waste their time managing your moneys. They would rather make their own.)

21. No one has accidentally transferred extra money to you or transferred money to your digital wallet by mistake. If you get such a call, please disconnect and do not engage. Likewise, if you get a call from someone claiming to be friends or neighbours of your parents (or any other relative), wanting to return a 'loan' owed to them through your PayTM, do not share your details and tell them that a

direction to that effect has to come from your own relative or friend, not from a stranger. Best is to disconnect the call immediately.

22. Someone might call you to say that your bank account or mobile numbers will be deactivated shortly. They may ask you to dial 9 from your own phone to verify. Please do not respond to any such call. There are legal processes for deactivating everything. It makes sense to learn about these processes and at any rate, they don't begin with a phone call.

23. If someone calls from LIC or another insurance agency, telling you that a certain policy is maturing and your bank details are required for funds transfer, please tell them that you will update the details directly either with your agent or on the company's own website.

24. Check your credit card unbilled transactions. One unique method being followed is that small transactions are being done every month. The victim does not find out about these until a long time.

25. Let's understand **Digital Arrest**. If you have a police officer or customs official on the video call, and they are telling you that you cannot go anywhere from the video call until they have completely investigated your "crime" (whether it is a drugs parcel or terrorist having a mobile phone on your Aadhaar, doesn't matter), disconnect the call immediately and block the numbers. This is not police protocol. This fraud of holding a victim on a video call and coercing/convincing them to pay a 'fine' to avoid going to jail for a 'crime' is called digital arrest.

26. If you are playing an online game and someone offers to sell you their account or buy yours, don't do it. In most cases, it violates the game's terms of service. But more importantly, you do not want to have financial transactions with anonymous entities. – Tip shared by Ahaan Dutta

27. If you have matched with someone on a dating app, and you decide to meet at an eating joint, ensure that you see the prices before your order. There are two kinds of scam here - one, the café sets up fake profiles to invite people to a date. Then, no one turns up, making the person feel as if they have been stood up. The second is that the food bill is exorbitant. It makes sense to google "restaurant name + dating scam" before deciding on a venue for a date.

28. Income Tax refunds come to your bank account directly. You are not asked to click on any link.

29. At this time, traffic challans can only be filled in the court. A new scam type, where an SMS is received to pay challan online, has been reported by some people. Do not click on any link for paying traffic challan online.

30. A new type of scam is where you are sent a new mobile phone and asked to transfer your SIM to this new device to avail an offer. It could be a new credit card, a new deposit scheme, or other kinds of financial returns. Even a closed group investment opportunity.

31. If you are responsible for a company's online transfers, ensure that you take a daily cash statement from

each bank that you are a part of. Many small companies are finding that payments are happening from their accounts without OTP. As always, it is a good safety practice to add the additional layer of fixed deposit to current account funds.

32. No phone number begins with a special character. Do not dial bank numbers or delivery boy numbers that do not start with a legit digit. All numbers that start with # or * are codes that tell the phone to do something.

33. There is no challan/traffic fine pending on your vehicle. Go to the authorised government website. It lists all traffic fines pending against your vehicle. Do not trust any other website, link, or app.

34. If you get a marriage/wedding invite/invitation on Whatsapp, even from a friend, it is advisable to not open it. Cases of fraud due to wedding invites and traffic challans have grown disproportionately. Extend that to ANY invitation. Encourage your friends to send text invitations to things they want you to attend.

35. If you get a parcel, first, please check that it is something that you have actually ordered. Do not accept anything in your house and do not honour a Cash on Delivery order without checking where you ordered it from.

FOUR

Blackmail and Physical Crime

With deepfakes, we will soon see a rise in the number of cases of blackmail, physical crime, and extortion.

1. Do not discuss your family composition, especially the number and ages of children on a public platform or public place or over the phone. Don't comment on a Facebook group of 10,000 members - "How cute! My grandson is 8 years old too!"

2. This is basic, yet ignored by so many people all the time - cyber love is great. No pictures, please. Your partner might be safe. The platform isn't. The device may not be.

3. Do not discuss financial information in a public place. Never over the phone or on social media.

4. Even if you trust them implicitly and have worked with them for long, keep your personal financial information on a need-to-know basis only, for everyone.

Same for your relationship status.

5. Deepfake is real. If you get a video call from your dad telling you to come with this uncle or aunty because he is in the hospital, call your dad directly to find out if he is ok. If his phone is unreachable, do NOT go with the person.

6. In a public forum, NEVER share your personally identifiable information like home town, name of school, college, employer etc. These are used for phishing.

7. The old method of passcode still works well. With each member of your family, have a safe "Passcode." If your mom texts you to reach a place urgently, if you get a kidnap call, first get calm, then ask to speak to your family member. Once you do, ask them for the family passcode. Only your family member will know the passcode. Not the deepfake.

8. Keep your "Locate My Phone" and "Last Seen" on messaging apps like WhatAapp active. There are many people who have been saved by this one thing alone.

9. This is really important. Educate your children that if someone says they have compromising pictures or material on them, the right thing to do is to come to you. The absolutely wrong thing to do is to give in. In this day and age, many young people are being sexually and financially abused through the threat of a compromising video or picture. Nudes being leaked are no big deal. There is nothing to worry about. Then, tell yourself the same thing.

10. Do not give your phone to strangers who are in distress to "make a call." Ask them for the number they

want to dial, ask the name of the person at the other end. Then, make the call for them, and remain there while the conversation happens. Do not let them touch your keypad or move away from you while talking. Malware can be loaded on phones rather quickly – within 20 seconds, by some accounts.

https://www.youtube.com/watch?v=tmHI-uT2McI

11. In public places, please keep your Bluetooth turned off. It is possible to keep it linked to your headphones, but one needs to take a decision on whether the risk is worth the comfort. **Google Blue Bugging.**

https://www.youtube.com/watch?v=p4VF8HMCK0I

12. If you get an online order delivered to your house, always check that it is something that you actually did order. Do not turn on appliances or devices that you have not ordered. This could have tracking or listening devices, or, worse, could be stolen property that can be traced back to you.

FIVE

Political Manipulation

Let's consider a simple question – if social media companies like Facebook and Twitter decide who the President of the United States should be, is the United States still a sovereign nation?

Thanks to Cambridge Analytica and Twitter Files, we now know the extent to which these social media giants have tried to influence presidential elections – and this is only what is in the public domain.

But it is also true that these projects do not succeed because of big tech or big data. They succeed because of individuals who, when faced with a view that supports their bias, hit "like" instead of "hide."

As we know all too well, Imperial colonisation started with trading companies. The East India Companies were traders. They did not want political or military power, or so they said. We all know how that story ended.

It is not just that we have evidence of election tampering. It is also that in 2019, the then CEO of Twitter, Jack Dorsey, refused to appear before the Indian Parliamentary

Committee. It is possible for Big Tech to undermine the sovereign power of countries, because they control what the citizens think, how they will act, and what they will believe.

Of all the risks, this one is the most life changing for the multitudes. We already know what happened when specific leaders were chosen by countries.

The worst part about political manipulation is that it is insidious. It is invisible. And it gives us, people like you and me, the illusion of choice. We *think* we are making conscious decisions, but we are watching what we were meant to watch, getting the data that is intended for us, and 'independently' arriving at decisions that someone wanted us to take.

This is the most important part of this book. Of all things, as we Indians know, political freedom and independence, is the most fundamental.

Here are the tips to protect yourself from being a Big Tech Controlled Mind.

1. Do not post political content on social media. Do not participate in political debates on any social platform.

2. Do not click on political content on social media.

3. Get your news from multiple credible sources. Almost all mainstream media today displays some form of bias. One way to balance this is by reading from a variety of sources. For research papers, go to the original report and check out the sample size, methodology, etc.

4. Social media will share political content based on your browsing history. Do NOT fall for this clickbait. Social media is not the place to read news or get political updates. Ideally, do not read news stories while browsing social media sites.

5. Do not join protests based on social media posts. This applies to both physical and virtual protests and events. Do

not participate in Tweetstorms, sign political petitions, join candle marches, et al. If you find yourself drawn to a cause, sit back and evaluate. A good starting point would be to understand the perspective of the opposite side.

6. Social interactions and friendships – always above political stance. Whether we like it or not, technology is being used to not just influence, but actively create our political identity. The only way to not fall prey to this blatant manipulation of the mind is to not use technology to create a political opinion. Value friends more than political affiliations or opinions.

7. Fact-check everything. Then fact-check again. Biden and Trump both would not have been elected if Americans had not used social media for political information. (and this is only what is in the public domain).

8. When faced with a news item (the government is trying to kill the forests) - Always ask questions from the other side - Why is the government doing this? Who will benefit if the proposal goes through? Who will benefit if the proposal fails? Who is bringing the money to the table? Why? - These four questions are enough to help you see through most movements, protests, and 'Save the World' campaigns. Take a well-informed decision.

9. If you find your thoughts moving towards an 'Us vs Them' perspective, there is a very good chance that you are already being brainwashed.

Fear of elements within our society is necessary for colonisation to take place.

10. Please pay attention to manifestoes. Vote based on manifestoes. Ask questions about the promises made in previous manifestoes.

11. The best place to express your political opinion is inside the polling booth.

12. And finally, the most important tip is this:

NEVER Divorce Common Sense.

If it doesn't make common sense, it doesn't make any sense.

SIX

Cyber Bullying

Cyber bullying is using technology to, well, bully another person.

All of these actions come under cyber-bullying:

Trolling - posting an insulting message/comment.

Cyberstalking – when someone follows all your online activity. The stalker may or may not comment on or like your posts.

Doxing – Releasing personal details (like address, real name, email id, etc.) of a person on the internet for everyone to know.

Rumour mongering – The oldest kind of bullying finds its online cousin. As the name suggests, in this case, the bully spreads false and malicious rumours about the person.

Exclusion – When one person is not invited to WhatsApp groups, not tagged in photos, and otherwise kept out of communication loops on social media, messaging apps, etc.

Sadly, most victims of cyber bullying are children or teens. This means that this section is useful for both parents and children.

1. While playing online games, if you do not know the other players personally, do not say anything that is not related to playing. Within the game, do not use terms like "Stupid, why didn't you cover me?" or any other derogatory term. You don't know who is on the other side of that screen and how they will react to your words.
2. Try and play online games with friends you know personally.
3. This is a no brainer, but if you are playing in a group where some of you know each other and some team members are random strangers, do NOT take the real name of anyone.
4. **To the child/teen:** The BEST defence against cyber bullying is parents. They may get mad at your black nail paint or blue hair colour, but they WILL protect you if you are ever being cyber bulled. There are rules against cyber bullying in most schools and in cases where expressly hateful comments are posted, legal recourse can be taken. The most logical way to deal with cyber-bullying is by talking to the families and explaining how a certain behaviour is affecting another person. So, please talk to your parents when you are feeling stress because of what your friends are doing – online and offline. They have twice the experience you have of

being a teen – both of them were teenagers. They will know what to do.

5. **To the parents:** When your child or teen shares something related to cyber bullying (or any bullying), STOP whatever you are doing and LISTEN. Validate the child's feelings first. Don't cross question. Don't get details. Just listen and validate. THEN, after the child has shared completely, only then, start taking notes and asking for more details where relevant.
6. **Parents:** Periodically, talk to your children about their online activity. Keep an open space at home.
7. Bullying sometimes leads to physical hurt. But mostly, its about emotional hurt. Understand and manage your emotions. If you are an adult going through cyber bullying, take help. There are many healthy ways to deal with bullies. One of the best quotes read as a child helps me decide what to do in such situations:

"Don't accept unacceptable behaviour."

8. No matter how "chill" and "private" your WhatsApp or other private group is, never do any of the following on it:

a. Share someone else's personal information, including their email id or phone number.
b. Say anything, no matter how much in jest, that can be disrespectful or illegal. "I meant that in jest" is not a legal defence and you do not want to be on that side of the table.

c. Make any reference to any illegal act. “You are a nigga”, “We will deal with him/her." – Do NOT. There is no point in creating digital evidence that could ruin the rest of your life.

9. Every time you are writing, imagine that the reader is standing in front of you. Be respectful and polite. The anonymity granted by the internet allows us to be rude and angry. It is NOT ok. That is bullying. Many cyber bullies actually think they are doing this “for the greater good.”

10. One person’s cause is another person’s terrorism. Anything, no matter how universal it appears to you, is NOT universal to everyone. This includes but is not limited to:

a. Healthy eating
b. Environment
c. Education

- you get the picture.

The only person whose conduct you are responsible for, is yourself. And perhaps your immediate family. You do not need to correct anyone else’s thoughts, improve their knowledge, or expose their ‘attitude issues’. You are not a social reformer. You are a human being.

11. Cyber bullying is a legal offence in India. (and in many other parts of the world). However, much of this cyber bullying is done and tolerated in a state of ignorance. The bullies do not understand the effect their words have on others, and the bullied do not know that they can actually take action – both regulatory (in a school/college/office, within the organisation) and legal, in

these cases.

12. First, do not participate in a discussion where you can see that people are being disrespectful to each other. Then, if you do get involved, never say anything that you don't want read out in a court of law. Third, at the FIRST instance of being bullied, call out the bully and tell them that this behaviour is not acceptable and comes under cyber bullying.
13. If you are being excluded, do exactly what you would do if you were being excluded in a physical space – the playground, for example.
14. If you are being cyber stalked, collect evidence and then take expert opinion on how to proceed. Stalking is a serious offence.
15. Unlike other tips in this book which are straight and directive, this tip is advisory. It may not work for everyone.

What to do when your child or teen comes to you with a cyber bullying experience?

- Start by listening completely. Drop whatever you are doing. Just sit next to your child and listen. Let them talk as much as they want to.
- Then, give a message of reassurance that is empathic and not dismissive. Not "Arre! This is hardly anything. We can deal with it in a jiffy!" but, "I understand this has been a bad experience. We will get through this. Let's **work together.**"
- The reason you have to say '**work together**' is that part of getting out of a situation is giving the child the toolkit

to manage this. Make them feel a part of the process.

- Take all details from the child. What, when, who, how, and if possible, why.
- If you know the other family very well, a chat between the parents might work well. If they are in the same institution, making a formal complaint might help. If neither of these is true, do go to the police. No matter what, do not normalise the bullying and tell your child "Hota hai – this happens all the time."

16. How to tell if I am a cyber bully?

This question is more important than it appears. Most cyber bullies would be shocked to know that someone thinks of them that way. So, here are two simple guidelines to ensure that you do not become a cyber bully. Old wisdom, always relevant:

- If you don't have something good to say about someone, stay quiet.
- If you won't write it and sign it, don't say it.

SEVEN

GENERAL TIPS

There are many ways for our data to be compromised. Compromised data, in turn, can be used in many ways. It can be used to steal our money or direct our minds. We have no way of predicting what our information can be used for tomorrow.

These tips are wide-ranging and help minimise the exposure of normal people like us to cyber and online crimc.

1. When giving out your data for "Registration" - ALWAYS ask:

a. Why is this being collected? (You don't need to give your email id and phone number to enter an event, buy something at a retail store, or meet a professional who does not need your personal data. In fact, the default state is to NOT share your data. So, always ask WHY they need to collect it. If the answer is - "We just need it", or "It's our process" - Leave. You are not missing anything in life.)

b. Where is this going to be stored? On the cloud? In your hard drive?

c. Who will have access to this information?

d. How will you protect it? What is the safety standard that you use to store your data? Who do you give APIs to?

Do NOT worry about looking awkward or odd. You need to be sure that they really need this info to complete your request, and that they are capable of safeguarding data that is owned by YOU.

2. If you are meeting an online friend for the first time, meet in a public place. Not at either of the homes, even if they say it's a get-together and many people are expected.

3. There are no miracle cures. No soulmate is dying to talk to you online. You have not won any lottery. There is no limited time opportunity to invest or get a job. No one has selected you for a job without an interview. No friend of yours is stranded and needs your help. Tax officers are not going to fine you. That new website does not sell everything cheaper.

4. When you are given a choice to log in using Google or Facebook, check carefully the data the site will get when you connect the two. Usually, it's fine. But check. And if you are uncomfortable, use an email id you have exclusively for these websites.

5. On Facebook, Google, and other platforms, go to your account and disable access to third-party apps that you are no longer using. Do this at least once every six months.

6. Do NOT use free Wi-Fi at any place. Use your own mobile data hotspot. This applies to airports, high-end hotels, cafes, and every other place. In India, data is really cheap now.

7. On any browser, log out, don't just close the tab or window.

8. Add your phone number to DND. Then, if you get a call or message, complain to TRAI for sure. You will notice that

the number of violators of DND will go down once you start complaining.

9. Subscribe to ***haveibeenpwned?*** With all your email ids. It is a service that tells you when your email id is a part of a data breach.

10. Keep an offline backup of all your data on a separate SSD or Hard drive. Do this periodically. Before every travel, ensure that you take a backup on a hard drive and leave that hard drive at home.

11. Charge your devices at home or use a personal power bank. Avoid public charging points. If using a public charging point, use your own charger with the plug inserted into the electric socket. Don't use the ones where only the charging node is visible to you.

12. Do not install any directory app that requires you to share your contact list with the cloud or with the developers of the app. You would not give your entire contact list to a stranger, would you?

13. While installing CCTV at home, try and get the storage on a local hard drive. Cloud storage of home CCTV footage is a vulnerability.

14. Do NOT choose childcare centres that beam images of your children over the internet for you to monitor them. If you can see them, so can hackers.

15. Your Date of Birth, mother's maiden name, first school, place of marriage, and other such details are also used as security questions in many applications. So, don't put this content on social media.

16. Don't give kids social media accounts, no matter how much they cry. Don't post pictures of children on social media, no matter how cute they are and how close the group is. The group is reliable. The platforms are not. A great way to ensure that children do not ask for or get

addicted to social media – is to ensure that one does not get addicted to these platforms themselves. If children see parents addicted to the internet, they will follow suit.

17. On social media, NEVER accept requests from people you do not know. This is how spear phishing is done. (a targeted email is sent to one person. This email is designed as per the usage behaviour and interests of that one person).

18. If your computer hangs often and this has started recently, get a thorough scan done.

19. If you find yourself wanting to play a game or an app when you should be doing something else, it's time for a digital detox. Do not take this lightly. All addiction leads to financial loss and loss of quality of life.

20. Hospitals are, unfortunately, one of the most vulnerable data centres.

If you can, use the services of doctors who own their data centre or keep patient records locally.

When choosing a diagnostic centre, choose one that stores data locally. Indian law requires medical practitioners to retain details of treatment for about 2/3 years, but there is no need to put this data on the cloud.

Avoid putting medical data of any kind on the cloud as far as possible. You can also ask for your data to be deleted after 3 years. In multiple cases, the Honourable courts have held that the patient is the absolute owner of their medical records.

21. While installing an app, check the permissions it is seeking carefully. A photo editing app does not need to read your SMS. When in doubt, do not install.

22. Use browsers that don't ***dial home[1]*** - send data to their developers. Brave and DuckDuckGo are both great mobile browsers.

[1] Dialing home is when a browser sends user data to its makers. Edge and Chrome send the most data to their creators. A simple Google search will lead you to industry analysis of dialing home by browsers.

23. If your phone is using up battery very quickly or is heating up, immediately uninstall ALL financial and social media apps from it and change your passwords. The phone may or may not be compromised, but changing your credentials will save you proactively.

24. Every time you enter a loyalty program, your personal details are stored with that company. IF the servers of that company are ever compromised, your identity and personal information is compromised too. Be mindful of which loyalty programs you are a part of. If you'd like, do check the data security history of the company. If the company has a history of not reporting leaks until an independent researcher or government flags it, a good idea would be to skip it.

25. If you receive a call from someone and they ask you to press any key on your keypad – for any reason at all – do not. They might pretend to be government, police, tax, or telecom officials. The call may be related to illegal activity on your name, or it might be a case of SIM card upgrade. Either way, do not press any key on your keypad while the call is going on. Any key pressed on the keypad which is not done as part of IVR is you giving your phone a command.

For instance, *401#, followed by a mobile number, leads to unconditional forwarding of all your calls to the said mobile number.

26. Recently, the Government of India has launched a service that allows you to report the number from which a fraudulent call has been placed. The Department is also

enforcing other measures to ensure that telephones cannot be used for spamming or illegal activity. Here are some useful links for India:

To report spam: SMS to 1909

To report an actual financial crime: Call 1930

To report a suspected fraud even if you saved yourself: https://sancharsaathi.gov.in/sfc/

More citizen services here: https://sancharsaathi.gov.in/

27. Keep the IMEI numbers of all your phones handy with you. If the phone is lost or stolen, IMEI numbers are the hardest hardware evidence to remove. The phone may be recycled, but it will likely not be used again if you report the IMEI numbers.

To get the IMEI number of your device, press *#06* on your device while it is NOT on any call. The 15-digit IMEI number will appear on screen.

28. In the unlikely event of a phone being stolen or lost, you can do the following:

1. Report the stolen mobile and get an FIR number (this is required in case your phone is subsequently used in a crime and you need to prove it was not with you at that time).

2. Report the mobile number on this DoT website: https://ceir.sancharsaathi.gov.in/Request/CeirUserBlockRequestDirect.jsp

3. If you have a Google account on your Android Device, use the Find My Device service from Google. It is a basic MDM (Mobile Device Management) that allows you to at least remote wipe (remove all content) your device. A similar service exists for Apple users too.

References

- Lady loses 27 Lakhs to foreign friend on Facebook – Mumbai.
- https://www.livemint.com/money/personal-finance/pune-man-loses-rs-2-1-crore-to-online-fraud-how-to-keep-yourself-safe-from-cyber-criminals-11704364702195.html
- https://www.indiatoday.in/india-today-insight/story/from-the-india-today-archives-2023-online-fraud-a-raging-menace-2484367-2024-01-04
- Crime in India Reports – 2020, 2021, 2022.
- Daily releases from I4C
- Media interviews and releases by respective government and police bodies.
- Press Reports of cybercrime from various news publications.

Epilogue

This book is based on real behaviour exploited by hackers and criminals.

Thank you for reading. I hope it helps you, or someone around you, avoid a fraud.

Let's Connect!

Email: authnidhi@gmail.com

Instagram: @authnidhi